650

POEMS
of
CHILDHOOD

JOAN WALSH ANGLUND

Harcourt Brace & Company

San Diego   New York   London

With love for Fran Maclay and the Clymer family

Library of Congress Cataloging-in-Publication Data
Anglund, Joan Walsh.
Poems of childhood/Joan Walsh Anglund.
p.   cm.
ISBN 0-15-262961-0
1. Children—Poetry.   I. Title.
PS3551.N47P64   1996
811'.54—dc20   95-30937

First edition
A C E F D B

Printed in Singapore

Also by Joan Walsh Anglund

From my window I can see
the whole world waiting there for me.
A fresh, bright day beginning, new.
Oh, come and look!
I'll share with you.

Spring! Spring!
It's lovely spring!
The tulips nod,
the robins sing.
The grass is green,
sweet breezes blow.
The apple blossoms
spill like snow.

A sea of gold
the jonquils are,
and joy surrounds us,
near and far!

So many children just like me,
in far-off places across the sea,
living and learning and busy every day;
I wish I could know them,
I wish we could play.
So many children I have yet to greet.
Each one a friend, if we could just meet.

I'm sitting very quietly,
I'm sitting very still,
upon a big rock
on a grassy hill.
I'm sitting all alone
where no one else can see,
because if I'm careful,
a bunny visits me.
From out of the bushes
he often comes for lunch.
He eats tender grasses
with a nibble and a crunch.
He wiggles his nose
in a very funny way,
then with a sudden hop,
my bunny's gone away!
I'm sitting very quietly,
as silent as can be,
because if I'm careful,
a bunny visits me.

I look at the world
  and I think to myself:
    What a wonderful place to be,
      with mountains and valleys
        and flowers and trees,
          there's such beauty for all to see.

A symphony of lark song,
a busyness of bees,
a farewell of snowflakes,
a freshening of breeze,
a companionship of butterflies,
a triumph of sun,
a trumpeting of daffodils,
with such has springtime won.

Sometimes the wind is wicked;

it's as naughty as can be.

Just yesterday it came along

and stole a kite from me.

It snapped the string I held so tight

and pulled and tugged with all its might

until it lifted kite and all

above the roofs and trees so tall.

Then, not content with even that,

it came right back and stole my hat!

All among the dewy green,

a little someone I have seen—

a furry person, very small—

scampers, quick, along my wall,

darts and hides without a sound,

pokes out her head and looks around,

picks up a seed and with a squeak,

slips through a hole where I can't peek.

I'm angry. I'm furious!
I'm really really mad
'cause someone broke my airplane,
the only one I had!
Someone was so careless,
someone was so bad,
I'll hold my breath
till I turn blue!
You've fixed it?
Oh! Thanks, Dad.

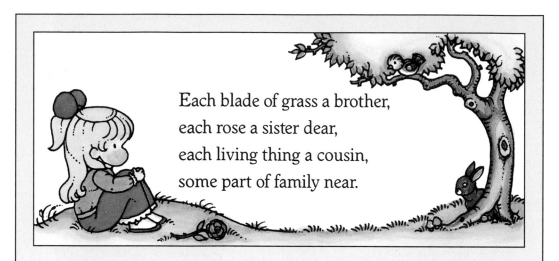

Each blade of grass a brother,
each rose a sister dear,
each living thing a cousin,
some part of family near.

In a movable house I carry about,
I'm cozy within and so safe without.
Many may knock at my door with a grin,
but, oh no, my friends,
no one gets in.

A clock is a circle
with numbers around.
It ticks and it tocks
with a most pleasant sound.

Its two little hands
so steadily go
around and around
to let us all know
just when to get up
and when we should dine—
what hour to dress,
what hour to recline.
It's busy all day
and it's busy all night,
counting the minutes
and keeping things right.
Because of its help
we're not tardy, not late.
We're awakened at seven;
we're in bed by eight.
Our appointments are kept;
there is time for each task.
Our lives are in order.
What more could we ask?
A clock is a friend,
so steady and true.
Without her to guide us,
what would we all do?

Balloons are floating
everywhere,
presents are waiting
on table and chair,
pink cake and ice cream
are ready to share—
a birthday is happening,
and I'm going to be there!

At sunset they say, "Time for bed!"
But wouldn't it be nice instead
for them to let me stay awhile
to see the moon's great grinning smile,
to hear the cricket's last faint song
and chase the fireflies along,
to watch as stars first start to peep
before I'm hurried off to sleep?

Yellow, amber,
orange, and red,
the leaves are sprinkling
on my head.
The air is merry
and all the trees
now stand in gold
up to their knees.

It is very easy to hurt a friend
and it takes so long for a heart to mend.
So let us be careful of words we say
and be kind to each other
as we work and play.

Even the smallest acorn may one day
be the father of great forests!

Three little friends
went down the dark street.
Whom do you think
they happened to meet?
A scowling witch
and a big black cat,
a spooky ghost—
now just think of that!
So they ran right home
without trick or treat,
'cause it's scary sometimes
on a Halloween street!

Red is an apple.
Green is a tree.

Yellow is a warm sun,
shining down on me.

Blue is an ocean
in which I swim and play.
Purple is a mountain,
so high and far away.

Pink is a flower,
blooming in the park.
And orange is my pumpkin,
smiling in the dark!

The golden leaves
flew through the air.
The trees were cold;
their boughs were bare.
But snow blew in
one frosty night
and dressed them all
in robes of white.

Once there was a snowman,
so big and tall and wise,
made from a million snowflakes
that fell from out of the skies.

I played all day with my snowman;
we had such frosty fun.
But my friend went away—
he vanished—
with the rise of the morning sun!

Merry merry holiday!
Welcome, one and all!
Presents in the parlor
and holly in the hall.

Turkey in the kitchen,
children on the stair.
Stockings at the warm hearth
and Christmas everywhere!

We stayed too long;
our toes went numb.
The sun had set;
the dark had come.
The air was cold;
our breath made ghosts.
The snow put hats
on all the posts.
Our sleds were heavy;
across the hill
the town lights twinkled.
The night was still.

The moon came up.
We reached our gate.
Our mother called,
"You're home!
It's late!"

I'd like to ride a little cloud
all across the sky,
and visit with the birds up there
and watch the stars go by
and talk with the wise moon-man,
and before my trip was done,
I'd find out where the rainbows start
and what happens to the sun!

I hear the big storm
as he crashes about;
all through the treetops
I hear his loud shout.
He always sounds angry,
but I never know why,
as he rattles his thunder
and lights up the sky.
He's not the least quiet,
as guests ought to be.
No! He doesn't seem friendly
to Teddy and me.
So, we hide neath our covers,
all cozy and still,
till that grumpy storm's tired
and goes home past the hill.

Good night, good night,
and now to sleep.
The moon is bright,
the shadows deep.
The stars atwinkle
high above,
and all about us
love, sweet love.